Pitkin
County
Library

1 13 00

D0132259

120 North M
Aspen, Colorado 81611

811.54 P882
Powell, D. A. (Douglas A.)
Cocktails

WITHDRAWN

DATE DUE

JUL 3 1 2005	

GAYLORD — PRINTED IN U.S.A.

ALSO BY D.A. POWELL

Lunch

Tea

Cocktails

D. A. Powell

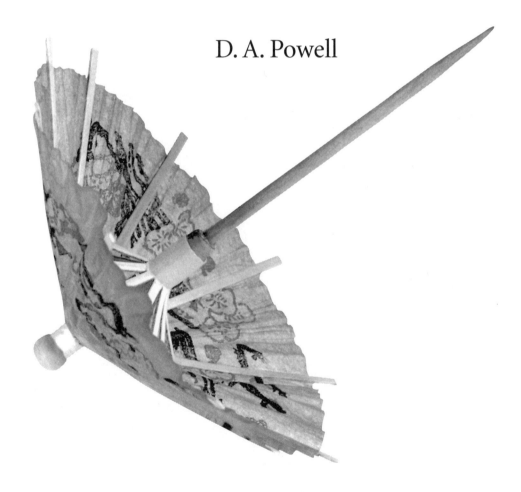

Graywolf Press

SAINT PAUL, MINNESOTA

Copyright © 2004 by D. A. Powell

Publication of this volume is made possible in part by a grant provided by the Minnesota State Arts Board, through an appropriation by the Minnesota State Legislature; a grant from the Wells Fargo Foundation Minnesota; and a grant from the National Endowment for the Arts. Significant support has also been provided by the Bush Foundation; Target, Marshall Field's and Mervyn's with support from the Target Foundation; the McKnight Foundation; and other generous contributions from foundations, corporations, and individuals. To these organizations and individuals we offer our heartfelt thanks.

MINNESOTA
STATE ARTS BOARD

NATIONAL
ENDOWMENT
FOR THE ARTS

Published by Graywolf Press
2402 University Avenue, Suite 203
Saint Paul, Minnesota 55114
All rights reserved.

www.graywolfpress.org

Published in the United States of America

811.54
POW
11.04   ISBN 1-55597-395-7

2 4 6 8 9 7 5 3 1
First Graywolf Printing, 2004

Library of Congress Control Number: 2003111078

Cover design: Kyle G. Hunter
Cover image: Parasol image copyright ©Hot Ideas/Index Stock Imagery

Acknowledgments

Some of these poems first appeared in the following journals: *American Letters & Commentary, Barrow Street, The Blue Moon Review, Bridge, Bombay Gin, Boomerang, Boston Review, The Canary, Chelsea, Chicago Review, Colorado Review, Columbia Journal, Columbia Poetry Review, Gulf Coast, Indiana Review, Interim, Iowa Review, Jubilat, Mary, NewMediaPoets, Pleiades, Prairie Schooner, Provincetown Arts, Shampoo, Solo, The Southeast Review, The Poker,* and *Xantippe.*

"[I was a priapic boy: the prow of a galleon]" appeared in the anthology *The Brink: Postmodern Poetry 1965 to Present* from Yeti Press in Kerala, India, 2002.

"[my lot to spin the purple: that the tabernacle should be made]" appeared in the anthology *Pushcart Prize XXVII* from Pushcart Press in Wainscott, New York, 2003.

"[12-line poem, seemingly out of place]" first appeared in *Modern Poetry in Translation, No. 15* in London, UK, 1999, as an untitled translation of Aleksandr Pushkin's "Мирская Власть." Perhaps this was not the worst thing ever to happen to Pushkin.

"[the ice hadn't cracked. stingy ground: frozen with its hoard of bulbs]" was included in the exhibition *Landscapes* at the Delaine Eastin Gallery in Healdsburg, California, in the spring of 2002.

Thanks to those who read and responded to portions of this manuscript while it was in process: John Isles, Kristen Hanlon, Rachel Zucker, Sam Witt, Carol Ciavonne, Rusty Morrison, Mary Wang, Ryan Berg, Julia Ward, David Bromige, Valerie Savior, Saskia Hamilton, and Jorie Graham.

For Christopher Fritzsche and for Christopher Patrick

Contents

Bibliography

Cocktails

. . . all the very gay places,
those 'come what may' places
where one relaxes on the axis of the wheel of life
to get the feel of life:
jazz and cocktails.

—*Billy Strayhorn, "Lush Life"*

 Mixology

Ho! stand to your glasses steady!
'Tis all we have left to prize.
A cup to the dead already,—
Hurrah for the next that dies!

—Bartholomew Dowling,
  "The Revel: Time of the Famine and Plague in India"

[the cocktail hour finally arrives: whether ending a day at the office]

the cocktail hour finally arrives: whether ending a day at the office
or opening the orifice at 6am [legal again to pour in californica]: the time is always right

we need a little glamour and glamour arrives: plenty of chipped ice
a green jurassic palm tree planted.   a yellow spastic monkey swinging

a pink classic flamingo impaled upon the exuberant red of cherries
dash of bitters.   vermouth sweet.   enough rye whiskey to kill

this longing: I take my drinks stiff and stuffed with plastic.   like my lovers
my billfold full of rubbers.   **OPEN**s my mouth: its tiny neon lounge

[this is what you love: more people. you remember]

this is what you love: more people.   you remember
to say "of all the men I know" and "your nice friend kimber"

but it wasn't always so.   living in a big shoe and knotslips
in your bed the size of taxes [or texas?   you don't read lips

as well you should]   some hearing loss due to family
in your ears: homilies and hominy and decidedly no harmony

no wonder *the bad seed* topped your list of favorite flicks
having that brood crush you down into the mattress: you kicked

one fell out and the other nine said "rollover, rollover"
who could go to sleep with the sound of music?   and the hot covers

now you only regret men unbedded.   unwedded to your cheek-y
desire to lift strangers from taxis.   or texas: why be picky?

but you've gone "gee" in your ratings: shirley temple and madeline
volunteer work.   neighborhood meetings.   you even bring the gelatine

[he would care for me as a stranger: courtesy clerk. so quick]

he would care for me as a stranger: courtesy clerk.   so quick
that I scarcely noticed how he handled.   my eggs.   tomatoes
household explodeables.   each within its own white skin
the safeway around.   parts of bodies kept from rubbing
into cheese.   bleeding into delicate figs.   time was I was

a nasty little bugger: took a bite of every grocery clerk
and put them all back.   rosy cheeks faced out: hiding
what I'd done to make them rotten: I could not see
a clump of grapes and not think "pesticide."   crossing items

off my list I'd drift through the frozen aisle to piped-in
air supply: *all out of love.*   all out of häagen-dazs.   unmoved
by the way he called me angel biscuits.   hostess cake
as he tucked a receipt for my muskmelon into my jeans

[writing for a young man on the redline train: "to his boy mistress"]

All the bodies we cannot touch
are like harps. Toucht by the mind

—Robert Duncan, "Fragments of a Disordered Devotion"

writing for a young man on the redline train: "to his boy mistress"
first to praise his frame: pliable as hickory.   his greasy locks waxy ears
I'll stop the world and melt with you brustling through a nearby headset

if I had time to ride this monster to the end I would: hung by handstraps
jostle through the downtown stations.   each stop bringing us closer
to what?   gether?   perhaps: or that exit of the tunnel where I look back

and *poof:* no lover.   men have led shameful lives for less proportioned fare
tossing greetings thick as rapunzel's hair: "anybody ever told you that you
[ugh, here it comes lads, stifle those chortles] resemble a young james dean?"

why *fiddle-dee-dee,* he bats his lids: the fantasy already turning to ruin
what if he debarked at my destination of pure coincidence?   followed
through the coppice of the square: fox and hound, fox and hound

I'd lead him on a merry chase: pausing every few: admire a fedora
check the windows of the haberdashers and cruise the sartorial shops
until I felt his winded breathing on my neck: yawned and departed again

we could while away the afternoon just so.   but at my back, etc

fresh and sprouting in chestnut-colored pubes is how I'd want him
not after the dregs of cigarettes.   the years of too many scotch sours
why, I wouldn't even know what to say to one who drinks scotch sours

except, "sir."   and "tough luck about those redsox" [which it always is]
now I've spent myself in lines and lost.   where is that boy of yesteryear?
let him die young and leave a pretty corpse: die with his legs in the air

[in the elegant days of downtown: we sunned on the porch]

in the elegant days of downtown: we sunned on the porch
no nose cancers grew.   no deep lines in our brows.   we lived

with a gassy dog.   tempestive guests.   a lawyer for a slumlord
a counselor next door and a trashman next door to that

the couch smelled where rotten pears had melted in the cushions
the coffee tasted burnt.   the whole house wept: a martini glass

was it the staircase that groaned?   boards under the carpet
that swamp cooler or the door that came unhinged at a touch

was it the picture of jesus over the mantel or the aceldama drops
from the red wax of the candles in their tarnished candelabras

iceblocks deliquescing in the kitchen.   pipes gargling the commode
that dog breaking wind in his sleep with the *hooty hoot* of a barn owl

perhaps someone's trick liquored up: stinking with navy stories
until we conked him.   rolled him down the steps in a drum

abundant as grass the graces touched us.   leaching through the walls
humming through oscillations of the sundering aluminum fans

in the wee light: a wilding song unsettled.   a bell for the coming mass

[gardenhose dilated with rain: a puff adder]

. . . when the water receded it left depressions
shaped like graves in orchards.

—*Tracy Kidder, The Road to Yuba City:*
A Journey into the Juan Corona Murders

gardenhose dilated with rain: a puff adder
so we retreat like tigers.   tails between our legs

summer: so crazy about peaches we're crazy
driving through orchards and the brown silt
clings to us.   flesh clings to pit: our hearts are woody

twenty-six bruised males planted face up
under the supplicant branches.   honey stench
something wormed hard into their boyish clefts

"when I was a tortilla salesman," I'm apt to begin
in the hum of pigs' blood and the sigh of cottonwood of

braceros with bedroom smiles and bad teeth who tooled
their names into their leather belts with the blunt tip
of a machete.   who harrowed bindweed and ragwort

and dropped their dungarees behind the flats of freestone
¿como?   how the eye drips with *corona* and prayers
mumble skyward: crows instead of kisses, *amigo*

[*amigo, n.*—friend, familiar, or an interjection like "halt"]

I too made love to *nameless male no. 17:* his hair curled around
his dagger tattoo suspended over his heart.   he said:

and I answered in the same tongue.   seedling
your roots exposed along with a chambray shirt: tugging
you out of the earth: naked.   trampled.   pulp.   scythe

I called you darling 14 ways.   I called you *peaches*

[winter moon summer moon budding moon barley moon]

a song of almanacs

winter moon summer moon budding moon barley moon
moon when the leaves are green.   moon when horns break off
the kindly moon the cooking moon moons for famine: big and little

a moon for raccoons a moon for the trees to pop.   chaste moon
the moon that makes eyes sore from the bright of snow
a moon sassafras a moon of ice a moon for awakening: a peach

moon of the terrible moon disputed.   returning geese scattered in formation
the oak the peony long night the storm the moon in the middle of summer
a trap a bone a hungry ghost   m [∞] n   the lightning the ripening berries

[a happiest harbinger to you: here spring]

a happiest harbinger to you: here spring
has a crocus to send out.   which is the parade
and hog day and cogitating bulbs in the temple of ground

your body is everywhere this fine day: a downy hare
a slender magnolia bud.   the whistle in pussywillow
in sanfrancisco the chinese and dragons hoot.   all about

scott: the easter of my astrological garden.   cherry blossom
pink and a hummingbird sprung from blue.   splinter
you're scott on limbs naked blooming.   spread your living arms

[chapt. ex ex ex eye vee: in which scott has a birthday]

chapt. ex ex ex eye vee: in which scott has a birthday
[*many happy returns of the day*, says piglet] & buys himself a puppy

soon the scent of burning leaves is too much.   hunting season
the crisp flannel air and hot oatmeal: instead of fishin'

crunching out through the yawping woods.   with his terrier
legs spindled as muskets.   his slight chest heaves.   his slender derriere

a pale chalkmark among the birches.   for a time he sits and smokes
scratching the curious brown dog behind its ears.   then snow

dusting down like dandruff on their collars.   they wait on haunches
listen for the woodchuck or roebuck: they have their lunches

and the whiteness covers them almost completely.   almost
far enough away from this moon and those rabbits and the geese

[dogs and boys can treat you like trash. and dogs do love trash]

dogs and boys can treat you like trash.   and dogs do love trash
to nuzzle their muzzles.   they slather with tongues that smell like their nuts

but the boys are fickle when they lick you.   they stick you with twigs
and roll you over like roaches.   then off with another: those sluts

with their asses so tight you couldn't get them to budge for a turd
so unlike the dogs: who will turn in a circle showing & showing their butts

a dog on a leash: a friend in the world.   he'll crawl into bed on all fours
and curl up at your toes.   he'll give you his nose.   he'll slobber on cuts

a dog is not fragile; he's fixed.   but a boy: cannot give you his love
he closes his eyes to your kisses.   he hisses.   a boy is a putz

with a sponge for a brain.   and a mop for a heart: he'll soak up your love
if you let him and leave you as dry as a cork.   he'll punch out your guts

when a boy goes away: to another boy's arms.   what else can you do
but lie down with the dogs.   with the hounds with the curs.   with the mutts

[12-line poem, seemingly out of place]

a bad translation of Pushkin, ending with a line from a John Waters movie

then the vehicular manslaughter took place: a tornado
of metal and suffering in the crosswalk: my god
he must have lost consciousness there where two marys
with very different handbags stood working

these days the block has its crossing guard: the mayor
sends volunteers in hats and sashes: to guard what?
can this bloodstained place be carjacked, eaten by rats?
will the dead like giants invade folks' imaginations?

or will the past reverse itself: a speeding ferrari
so that no lean body lies broken in the intersection
so that poor bastard isn't missed.   isn't starved after
by ladies, boys, wretches who holler *eggs, eggs, eggs*

[the mind of moss: sitting here by the reflecting pool]

the mind of moss: sitting here by the reflecting pool
hoping our shapes will never change.   as if

attention to form will save us from foundering
from cold cereal.   and from serious young men

who could forgive our weakening loyalties

water doesn't hold our place: one day
we set down the long russian novel we've been ~~living~~ [writing?]

and the names of the characters blur.   the plot
becomes completely twisted: the way we once forgot

the names of the 7 dwarves.   also the dog's birthday also
a luncheon with kind aunt sarah.   and when we return

a child has folded the pages into paper sailboats
look: little rudderless skiffs listing and drifting

time to abandon this silly regatta.   time to skip stones

[when you touch down upon this earth. little reindeers]

when you touch down upon this earth.   little reindeers
hoofing murderously at the gray slate roof: I lie beneath
dearest father xmas: will you bring me another 17 years

you gave me my first tin star and my first tin wreath
warm socks tangerines and a sloppy midnight kiss
I left you tollhouse cookies.   you left me bloody briefs

lipodystrophy neurosthesia neutropenia mild psychosis
increased liver enzymes increased bilirubin and a sweater
don't get me wrong: I like the sweater.   though it itches

but what's the use of being pretty if I won't get better?
bouncing me against your red woolies you whisper: *dear
boy:* unzip your enormous sack.   pull me quick into winter

[this little treatment has side effects: side effects]

this little treatment has side effects: side effects
including [but not limited to] poseidon emerging from the sea
striking his patinaed trident against the shore of my muscle
beach party: tremulant.   a quake.   a tension and slack in the arches

or the seawall inside me breaks: torrents.   did I mention horses?
they whinny snort and neigh up my pipes: herd music
and the squall that rocks my dandy timbers.   snaps my mizzen

the tablet I accept as a gift from god.   must be crushed
absorbed without food.   in this way it is like faith: senseless
yet entirely restorative.   mind you: the urge to crap is immediate

the black and red pill comforts me.   the yellow one
[I have to think: was that the one for sharon tate
in *valley of the dolls?*] induces dreams: I am hecuba
achilles.   three ugly fates in combination: spin measure cut

[*hope you like this new doctor:* rachel says in hopeful tones]

hope you like this new doctor: rachel says in hopeful tones
and I: *too early to tell.*   though hope does hover in my chest

certainly I've abandoned miss america-sized wishes:
world peace?   an end to hunger?   not while we consume, consume

I make hope the size of a bar of soap: hope-on-a-rope
like "hope there's not a spider in the shower this morning"

"hope some broadway producer brings back *starlight express*"
"maybe figs will be available fresh for a longer season

[without the global warming, I should add, in case god listens]"
and "maybe sheila e. will release a disc as good as *the glamorous life*"

my pulse drums too: a scant crew of leukocytes raise their tiny oars
these few who have not mutinied.   I want to lift their spirits

as we're crossing the equator: showered with a fine warm mist
I sing them a dusty springfield song.   soon the cabin's steamy

and we're *wishin' and hopin'* like there's no tomorrow.   but there *is*
already dawn: the passage safe: the mermaids beckon from the cape

—*for Rachel Zucker*

[my lover my phlebotomist. his elastic fingers encircle my arm]

my lover my phlebotomist.   his elastic fingers encircle my arm
psychopompos: he guides me away from my worldly woes.   his prick
cutaneous ➞ subcutaneous ➞ intravenous.   an underground passageway

I rise to meet him: engorged.   I wear a negligee and surgical mask
he's fat with smalltalk: "this fog" he says.   and "keeping busy?"   I am
I say "sometimes seems like all you want is blood."   he's sheepish today

maybe he wants to hold me to his brutal chest.   wrap me in gauze
press his coffee breath into my mouth.   our tongues: snakes: caduceus
then quickly the affair is over.   out on the street: my feet are swinging

my bloody valentine.   *sweet comic valentine.*

                                                        stay

                                                        . . . .

Filmography

If we go to the movies often enough and in a sufficiently reverent spirit, they will become more absorbing than the outer world, and the problems of reality will cease to burden us.

—*Quentin Crisp*

[robe and pajamas, steadfast and softer than anyone who touched me]

Papa's Delicate Condition (1963, George Marshall, dir.)

robe and pajamas, steadfast and softer than anyone who touched me

in the blear night dark: black your spine a musty bible.   we sway together

wrinkled lovers with tousled hair—a cocktail in hand—a pillow drenched in sweat

snowdrifts of terrycloth soaking where I spilled—mostly water: we measure
in drams and centiliters and shots: give me another, my sotted boys.   *roll footage:*

A LIFETIME OF HAPPINESS CONDENSED.   or, HAPPINESS OF A LIFETIME CONDENSED
we slip and slop and spill our soup—we pop our rocks—droop and droplet
flung over the back of the sofa: limp as a cashmere coverlet.   damp as a bloodclot

takes after his *(insert member here)* I heard of others.   but me?   I took after the dog

I don't know who brought these strawberry gin blossoms but surely they are mine
won't they look lovely next to the tv—the vd—the pictures of mom and pop

who fell in love with the circus.   brought it home every night: we cleared
beer bottles off the endtables: there, the stinko bears had room to dance their dance

PITKIN COUNTY LIBRARY
120 NORTH MILL
ASPEN CO 81611

[a mule-drawn scraper packed this earth: levees]

Ode to Billy Joe (1976, Max Baer Jr., dir.)

a mule-drawn scraper packed this earth: levees
mounded into ossuaries.   many a first flower
enjoyed the mud and let itself be plucked away
from church picnics.   the gathering of men in fields

"what do you remember about the first?"
"I remember the lids of his eyes.   the cup of his hand
under my head in the tall grass.   a sharp pain
in my guts: I remember saying the words:"

branching from the main body of the river
sumptuous sloughs and overflows: dissipating
potential floods.   neither depth nor velocity is attained

under the bridge.   half out of the moon.   overalls
bunched around our ankles.   a shame of a kiss
I cannot stay here: the river opens and swallows me

suppose the trawlers & dredgers continued the search
certain I had gone under a log: pinned.   the steady current
hounds sniffed under brush to catch my scent

miles downstream: lanterns swung out over the water
dreaming of my face.   the faces I had dreamt arose
on the roads: the coats of watchers.   uncloaking the new life

save those foxgloves pressed in the empty pages of genealogy
I lost the way back on purpose.   the delta empties into the sea

[19 lines]

Looking for Mr. G   bar (1977, Richard Brooks, dir.)

shapes repeat themselves.   and messages rewind
it's the answering machine you don't want to hear from

"I could never be kept," he says.   the fear of sobriety
wets his tongue: slips it into my ear with his number

sitting in prospect park bar: conveniently contained
by the lack of scenery.   his shorts creep up his leg

hand: too casual.   considering his inner thigh
parts of the same body arouse each other: kissing cousins

we all sleep with men who are not our lovers: economically
the barter is proposed: more drinks on the mastercard

the pitch and roll of a bed crosses my mind.   how to end
this groping beneath the formica table: nobody walks away

I used to wake beside the same body for years
its contours familiar: until it no longer suited

who knows where desire goes when it leaves the bed
a stranger comes to sit with me: we both light up

he's had a lover test positive.   his lips find my neck
his hand, his ass: I consider the risk of each part I want

there is a covert exit.   a cab waiting.   I sign for us both

[I was a priapic boy: the prow of a galleon]

Hook (1991, Steven Spielberg, dir.)

I was a priapic boy: the prow of a galleon
breaking through the warm caribée.   *avast*

the babysitter and I playing hide and seek
no search party: just him wrestling against me:

chained to the armoire.   a belt in my mouth
my knobby prisoner embouchured by his breathing hole

I was always a lost boy: swept into the nevernever
one among the private order.   who hung out

long after dark.   caught lightning bugs.   who
erected forts: buttressed against quizzical adulthood

who were hairless and soprano and angelically ungendered
whose dirtiest word was *balls:* those things we lacked

a strange kid would yank our underwear up our cracks
he and his nasty friends hid by the creek and smoked

"mama wants to know what's happened to your shirt
how come you come home without it?"

he said I had pretty hands.   as he tied them to the dresser

I was the boy who dreamed he could fly

I do believe   [clap your hands]   I do believe

[a boy at 15 can't be too tough: approximate masculinity]

My Own Private Idaho (1991, Gus Van Sant, dir.)

a boy at 15 can't be too tough: approximate masculinity
holds the daisy of his features clenched: raw and slight
a pebble of a rump.   scrawny his penis a plucked sparrow

his one talent: the ease of ejaculate.   not as handy as french

autos pass.   he shudders: imagines your bullet lodged

spiss and spiff: the way a hefty bag can contain him
along the highways speckles dot the grass.   is it easter?
he had that basket.   those lovely golden eggs

he had that blue-veined oyster you could cut with a knife

you had that *I'll take you as far as you dare* kind of look

when you pulled over: swirl of dust.   rubbish in safety orange

[every man needs a buddy. who'll do]

Making Love (1982, Arthur Hiller, dir.)

every man needs a buddy.   who'll do
when the wife has gone to the in-laws

the evening had already lowered.   he crossed
his legs in the manly way: outside

kids who could have been his yelled
"you're out."   and "no sir!"

eddie's two-bit country-singer looks: not my usual
dish of icecream.   and since he's mom's best friend's
live-in's daughter's hubbie.   the danger quickens

in the shed behind the natatorium: everyone knows
the device.   a meeting with the gardener's son

his voice rises and trembles: a steel guitar
the song of inalimental marriage.   he slobbers

on that part of me that is not woman.   his throat
an undergarment: silky and inviting

"man o man o god o man"   no confusion
about gender.   or the home he boomerangs to:
the good *she* who holds his place at supper

a man returns to his wife.   I understand the geometry
this is no equilateral triangle: compliments are exchanged

featherriver honkytonk: in the backrow I wait
so any life elapses under just such conditions:

no holidays.   no home.   relegated to odd nights
the frontseat of his car in lieu of the conjugal bed

he will never take his boots off

     *   *   *   *

"the act," he says.   meaning his career

[college roommate gone: his hamper full. I'll do us both a favor]

My Beautiful Launderette (1985, Stephen Frears, dir.)

college roommate gone: his hamper full.   I'll do us both a favor
sorting his socks like demented wife.   smoothing the pillowcase
its callipygous dent splayed bonewhite: spluttered where I laid him

what is a friend but a lover held at bay?   we find our quarry
want to tear each other: canines exposed.   our leashes tangle
grant us the safety of fenced-in yards: we worry the neighbors

love is seldom a dull chore: I know how to fold his t-shirts
how they smell before and after.   washing and tumbling
piggish delight the rooting after truffles.   whiff and snout

in his absence I build a model of him.   clothed in white undies
starched where he's starched and softened where he's soft
I use his favorite bounce.   bleach-free tide to hinder chafing

in separate rooms we count on our fingers the passing hours
we know the way each door swings open: how to find each other
agitating in the dark: sheets snaps elastic and those clumsy buttons

[the man in the front row: uniformed. ugly as my father the disillusioned]
Nashville (1975, Robert Altman, dir.)

the man in the front row: uniformed.   ugly as my father the disillusioned
train tracks ripped from the ridge.   fireworks over point charlie in his brain:

last night the barn swallows called me to the home place, he said.   I reckon he sleeps
in spangled drills and fire batons.   and in between a kind of peace: whippoorwills

there I sat and heard the call from the linseed-oiled perch of the choir: that was before
soldier pants parted the wings of their crotches or bluejays stole my trinkets

fiddles   grey geese   gingham   chokecherry jam   gnarled bark of a slippery elm

hills that knew us as they knew sunlight and the crash of hickory branches falling

now factories and country inns.   amusement parks.   dilapidated monuments
old ada on a respirator.   erma crazy.   tolbert weekending at the chicken farm

where we grew lanky and religious.   praised ammo and passed the lima beans
longing for dresden or paris (tennessee).   the far parthenon on a back lot in nashville

not this tarpaper hut in the holler where I was christened: *varmint* and *tater pie*
someone once said I called to mind a character in *snuffy smith.   god's little acre*

yes, it was just like that: bacon rind, wood stove, dynamite.   uncle burr kicked by mule
papa with a cottonmouth.   roe and ray in the pokey.   the night the kids got kerosene…

and: the last time I was in those hills I burned with fever.   drank water from an old jar
prayed in a tent in the woods until I felt the spirit leave me: in darkness, in utter dark

I can't imagine anymore.   dead hawk hung on the fence: fledglings in the snow
the rustle of some marcescent blossom: louisiana hayride, grand ole opry, WTNV

white lightning, daddykins, cemetery: *life may be a one-way street, but it don't worry me*

[morning broke on my cabin inverted. tempest in my forehead]

The Poseidon Adventure (1972, Ronald Neame, dir.)

morning broke on my cabin inverted.   tempest in my forehead
a fine kettle of fish, I'd tell myself, could I have pinpointed the date

marked SERO-CONVERSION in my pocket gregorian calendar.   [a guess?
sometime between the day lady day died and the day lady di died]

my lymphocyte is no gillyflower.   respiration no nightingale trilling in the dark
to those who hear crickets in sputum and the nightwind rasping in breath

I say: there is no positivity in being positive.   all that glitters is glitter

and so we have….   the climb:

first, think of all that can be jettisoned.   cumbersome clothes for example
[always the one thing I'd think of doing without]   when I was young

in borrowed 501s: had to have pants so someone could want to get in them
without boxers for weeks I could make do.   not beyond wearing slinky panties

if the occasion arose.   some drunk hetro plying me with schnapps: *dress up, doll*
what lies did he tell himself, biting his way down to that brass propeller shaft

also abandoned: retiring to miami [though I won't miss the guns or snakes]
or tel aviv [though I wouldn't miss the vipers.   or the snipers]

dreams of a hot husband in a hot tub who'd complain "honey, I shrunk my kids"
and drink fresca all day & rub my feet.   dreams of growing cantankerously old

shouting down the drainspout at a neighbor's brats.   clipping my ruby begonias
haggling over the price of nectarines at the pick 'n pack 'n scrimp 'n save

but climbing always: as up the trellis and overshrouding the eaves, wisteria
spreads in clusters of carcinoma-colored bells.   cascading epithelial light

up the spiral staircase of recombinant chromosomes.   no one wants in these genes
the double helix that swam through the treacherous night: aching to be held again

you couldn't know the disaster this voyage has been.   the *shvimen*, the *shvitzen*
yard by yard the little deaths accrued   [imagine your twin towers over and over and]

out: that glorious sky darkly hung with newspaper lanterns.   scalpel-shaped chimes

—what am I meaning to tell in this cramped space?   bubble suspended in glass—

the reckoning beyond this cargo hold.   dear god, who hears the pounding on the hull

[fortune drives a finned convertible: her blond wig shifts in the wind]

Mondo Trasho (1969, John Waters, dir.)

fortune drives a finned convertible: her blond wig shifts in the wind
in a lab somewhere: technicians spin me in centrifuge.   sudden skidmarks

doctors have no remedy.   they shine their bumpers and wax their hoods
every day I get a little more useless, starting with my shabby feet

the mind [precise once] spills on its favorite outfit: indelible inky wem
wish I'd get stains out.   the cloth of this *schmatte:* my pallium my hide

my, but the gutters bulge with dreck.   landscape flavor du jour: pigsty
no wonder the crones cackle behind my back: *what is it?* they blurt

: *a cake boy : a bone smuggler : a shim : a smurf : a rice and bean queen*
or a greengown?   a monosyllable?   a flesh broker?   a grape picker?   it could be

an ass hound.   a rancid flower.   maybe a street mechanic.   probably a peg boy
a flamer   a fister   a flipflop   a floozy   a fluffer   a fooper   a flyer   a frit

somewhere the shangri-las are singing an endless string of *no no no no no no*
somewhere happy bluebirds fly and even tired heels can take us home

[you'd want to go to the reunion: see]

Parting Glances (1986, Bill Sherwood, dir.)

you'd want to go to the reunion: see
who got heavy.   who got bald.   see

who has KS lesions on the face and listen
to the same old tunes: there'll be a dj sure as anything

you'd want to show off your boyfriend who's spare
as a girlscout cookie.   who drinks to excess

who is immortal who has not tasted
blood from a chalice.   the vampyre's kiss

and whosoever drinks from the cup, they'll tell you
everlasting: they'll say

where did you go when you were lively?
zippers, faces, exile, jackhammer, rawhide, wreck room, the stud

you dress in black leather: color of a cormorant
shared wardrobe passed among siblings.   a masqued ball

lazy last nights on earth: how long has it been since you laid in bed
all day during the workweek.   spewing and rattling like a baby

wearing the loose shift of your skin: all hallows eve
you spook your parents and run through the husks of the fields

remember that once, sneaking out into streets
you sought beyond the boundaries of board games:

life & sorry.   aggravation & trouble (the milton bradley version)
you allowed men to manipulate you.   and were gifted

good boy collectible.   good boy swappable
good boy in a kit with moveable parts: turn him over

see where he's been made.   you laid
in their toy chests.   keepsies

kids everywhere are called to supper: it's late
it's dark and you're all played out.   you want to go home

no rule is left to this game.   playmates scatter like breaking glass
they return to smear the _____.   and you're it

[so the theatre dimmed and reclined. cramped balcony rubbed against my leg]

Far From Heaven (2003, Todd Haynes, dir.)

> . . . leaving the movie before it's over
> with a pleasant stranger whose apartment is in the Heaven on Earth Bldg
>
> —Frank O'Hara, "Ave Maria"

so the theatre dimmed and reclined.   cramped balcony rubbed against my leg
nibbled popcorn from my buttery lap: what played that particular matinee?

not *les enfants du paradis*.   nothing noble: the re-release of *true grit* or *godzilla v. mothra*
it surprises me not that, years later, in a cassette of home movies, I see me skedaddling

eloped to the cinema— then: eloped *from* the cinema.   how I tore my dungarees
my drawers my shirt my fleshy bottom delicate membrane heart and pouty lips

lime-scented boy of jadite: the green son on a sunday.   fruit of the hidden orchard
to swear off the bottle and onto a stack of *cosmo*s and *esquire*s that it's true

while I collected ribbons for scripture [white ribbon = 5 verses, blue = 25 verses,
and 125 verses for red: color of the blood, my swollen mouth, my blushing penis]

the house teetered: whimpering for nails.   the wiring melted into a scouring pad
a spattering grease fire did what the termites couldn't: pickaxe, crowbar, battering ram

upstairs: the one parent slitting her skirt for sweet thing she brought back from market
the absent other: him at the oriental massage getting *jerkyjerky* and an icy finger up the bum

[I saw this movie twice.   both times I had to pee and missed this part: this parting]

now I wander into someone else's story: ghost light peering from the screen
a lambent young man opens his robe touching himself where he wants me to touch

take my hand and lead me stranger: hot, convulsing, delirious to taste of thy affection

[the atrium of the heart beckons with pendulous lips]

Fantastic Voyage (1966, Richard Fleischer, dir.)

the atrium of the heart beckons with pendulous lips
any seaman would point his submarine inside: sirens sing
an eye flutters.   strewn with carrion: the cliffs

pilot: could I go deep into the plasma of the sea
pull myself from the wreckage.   red tide, white squid
refractile bodies caught in this prismatic stream

surely salvation bilges.   suffers our immersion
as a macrocyte absorbs a viral fret.   into this deep
the whorl of shell and wave flash brilliant consecration

how the anvil beats within the limpet ear.   we drift
red sky at morning over the harbor: the hemoglobin
manta rays sensitive to the current's subtle shift

would the brain allow us entry like a rude thought docking
time to repair the nets and *overboard*   make for the tearducts
grow vast as a seamonkey: in tide pools.   sunlight draining

Bibliography

From the wide window towards the granite shore
The white sails still fly seaward, seaward flying
Unbroken wings

—*T. S. Eliot, "Ash Wednesday"*

[my lot to spin the purple: that the tabernacle should be made]
a song of Mary the mother

my lot to spin the purple: that the tabernacle should be made

with ten curtains of fine-twined linen and scarlet.   and the silk

and the hyacinthine.   even woven with the gold and the undefiled
which is white.   having the true purple for its veil

when the lot fell to me I took up my pitcher and filled it
took the purple upon my fingers and drew out the thread

in shag and floss: in coarse bottoms and in tight glossy skeins
the thrum did wind itself away from me

for a word had entered my womb and leapt inside me

I make the dark pillow where the moon lays its opaque head
I am the handmaid: pricked upon the spindle

the fine seric from the east was brought to me
soft and unfinished.   dyed in the tyrian manner

of purpura and janthina the violet snail.   cowrie and woodcock shell
the spiny hedgehog murex and the slender comb of venus

from betwixt my limbs arachnine the twisting issue I pulled forth

purple the night I felt the stab of the godhead in my side
purple the rot of the silk: its muscardine.   its plague

a raw tuft dwindles beneath me: I feel the tug of a day ravelling
even as such gloom as this winds tight around the wooden reel

would that a potion could blot out the host inside me
grove of oak, chestnut, willow.   a place of skulls.   succubi

a necropolis in me rises.   its colors mingle in the dark: aurora

spinster to throwster: purple my loom spread with the placenta cloth
I put a fine pattern to it: damascene sheaved and lilied

threads thrown in acute manner so that the bee rises on the border
the rose of sharon the cedar the camphire.   calamus and pleasant fruits

and these even dotted with locusts caddis flies and polyphemus moths
a fountain: a garden wattled with reeds upon the weaving

garden to be betrayed in?   a shadow against the breast of the tree

so the flox did luster in mine eye: in the cloth I beheld a fine water
as one might arduously with calander produce: the weft

a wave offering in my hands.   pin that pierces the body

over my lap a spreading wound of purple: purple that puckers and gathers
cloaking my folds of purple.   the swollen vein of a young boy's manhood

purple deep and hopeful.   a scar under the frenum.   a heavy prepuce

a caul.   an umbilical cord.   a wet sluice.   an angry fist.   a broken vessel
a bruise.   a blemish.   a raincloud.   a lesion.   a fissure.   tissue

the ends I took up and selvaged.   this veil shall not fray

and vast the warp of the cloth.   sea of galilee.   tigris euphrates and jordan
flow not as wide as my great bounty: undulant sky above my loom

the shuttle through me: a lance in my side.   a heave in my bowels
how will the temple receive my gift: scab of purple.   pustule.   genitalia

[and a future who? unfurls above the altar]   the thread the thread the thread

[unsheathed the sword and cut the veil. visible the planet red]

a song at the circumcision

unsheathed the sword and cut the veil.   visible the planet red
he wrapped in cloth: a loaf in offering.   stained: they crushed his grape
now wine trickles from the vats and the barnfloor aches its charge

nectar and pollen pend upon the purpled crown of his stamen
bees encircle the bracteal stalk.   goldfinches: thistledown in their beaks
tanned youths track his scent: rutting bucks with antlers locked

this spillage a petite suffering: sap droplets glister earthward
row that pules and groans to drink.   a pail a pyx a sacred cup
we sip we take our meal and tremble to have this blessing

bloodshed   tender mouths   the philtrum [indentation over the lips
where the seraph's appendage brushed us]   rent garment   skin of silk

a torn membrane makes a fine harp.   we call the sung phrase *ligature*

my love doesn't wind his body in a cloak.   he rears as a lion to the kill
statuesque: a harrow in the field.   the masses venerate his stook
from the steeple skyward reaching peal of bells: lauds and matins

as an athlete wrestles with angels: insists his solid body into aether
so the aether accepts him.   an abraded sky reveals its penetralia

this disquieting dawn the color of festering scabs: a cut that cannot suture
where the banding cloth releases: dehisced petals.   abandoned garments
these naked fishers cast papyrus nets.   this skin the shroud of waking:

46

[he tastes the air with his tongue. his eyes a gory kitling]

a song of John the Baptist, at the river

They shall take up serpents; and if they drink any deadly thing, it shall not hurt them;
they shall lay hands on the sick, and they shall recover.

— Mark 16:18

he tastes the air with his tongue.   his eyes a gory kitling
his glory: a copperhead's venom.   hemotoxic: eating corpuscles

corpus   redeemer   light   the risen   paraclete   and vine

in the crumpled tissues: moulting snakes tonsure themselves
their papery cowls rattle against the cattails and rushes

at the riverbed colubrid we flurry and wash: nest of vipers
unloosing the latchets of our shoes.   ankles sinking to mud

this canebrake divides and admits us.   reticulated leaves of orchis
erupt in marbled turrets: dry seed spurtles before us on the ground

the musk   the wood   viscosity   the damp   the *the*   the plague
a longing   breech   a rise to cataracts   oratory   anaphylaxis
houseled the heart   unburdened   the chorus   intemperate   unbound

he enters my basin and I swathe his swollen hood.   I bathe his skin
covering the body as rash.   open-lipt praise: I give.   to the wept chancres
[and the ones who kneel in the brush are watching bent and lusting]

filled on every side by his exuviae: through the shunt   the heparin lock
catheter   sigmoidoscope   endoscope   intubation   viaticum
I would gladly tear my own shroud at his command: be smeared

& rip.   popped discards: condoms glued to levees.   marking the trails
motocross bikes offroad vehicles and thongs have pressed the path

into the runnel clay.   you can't lose yourself in the floodplain:

go on down: to the wooded reach.   affuse yourself in lymph serene

trouble the water.   trouble the sedge the shore the weeds

down from your loft to the rippling issue.   on your knees unraveled
[aren't I?]   bending to the serpent twisting undulating coiling   [charming?]

shed   flayed open   winding through these grass and fear no deadly hand

[my riches I have squandered. spread with honey]
a song of the prodigal son

my riches I have squandered.   spread with honey
the arval bread in my pocket and nary a farthing

lived for a spell among roaches in a rickety squat
between the alcohol detox and the catholic church

peeled my plump white bottom.   a sauvignon grape
[now exsiccated: the wizened sultana makes no golden cake]

crouched in the gulleys.   wiped with leaves
cooked roadkill: topped with government surplus cheese

snuck in underage at club 21 (2121 21st street, long gone)

wastrel opal-throated bird: a moulting quivers along the pinion

I fear my mucus: its endless volume and amorphous shape
a demon expelling from my lips.   the moon wags its tongue

each dull morning the mirror imagines me a future: older
misshapen forest: stinging adder and sprawling spider

the way to haven seems interminable.   I creak and shuffle
listen, you wilderness: make plain and let me pass

[strange flower in my hands. porphyry shell. clipped wool]

a song of John the Divine with the Holy Prepuce, as in the vision of St. Birgitta

strange flower in my hands.   porphyry shell.   clipped wool
all the dark caves that beckon and terrible mud chambers of the wasp

I touched the raphe of your skin where once it had seamed to you:
amethyst jewels on your crown.   a skullcap upon the crozier of your loins

the old wet clothing of trees lies on the forest floor: naked world
spreading underbrush and tendrils of the new vines moist

once, I buried the soft body of you in my mouth.   licked that hurt place
where they'd cut you   [so long ago: you had put that infancy away]

you grew large inside me.   gifted my lips and throat with a swirling galaxy
milk of the nightsky.   balm from the trembling branches of the poplar

explosion of pale confetti signaling the new year.   the wine is bubbly
the bread, a generous slice.   I will make a ring of this covenant.   I will

bed thee down in a pasture and make a berm of your torso.   I am the marsh
above, a dipper pours thick liquid of your veins: cold now catch you I do

[they hear the clapping of the bell and are afraid]

a song of Lazarus the leper

they hear the clapping of the bell and are afraid
houses untenanted: bedslops spill from the windows
a clump of myrtle.   a scarlet ribbon against the jamb

look to the threshold: house of figs and of affliction
we whom you loved is sick.   maculed and papuled
our extremities knotted and breaking: the cypress bends

we was a beautiful lad once: not putrefactive nor foul
not blistering in the lips and nose.   not punctate: spots scaling
not mammillated with boils.   nor carbuncled.   not ulcerated

we also wore purple and byssus: we had carousing arms
jeweled and sexy.   required no nurse to dress we sores

and we'd easily slake: undeformed, without, *immaculato*

[torch to the stubble of the fields: the harvest has ended]

a song of Mary the Magdalene

torch to the stubble of the fields: the harvest has ended
in the black turf the last cinders wink and loll: the sentries sleeping

remember a time when grain beetled from its stalk.   a fit of ripeness
my body laid out in sheaves to be bound and threshed: broken chaff

all able plowmen leaned their weight upon the till.   furrowed maid
you see how the wheat was bundled: each season, more vetch more tares

untended the parcel fostered scrannel straw.   clods and shale and stone
nipples an earlobe an armpit: in town the statuary already crumbled

the new seed germing: gifting in the storehouse.   comb of honey
a jar of fragrant oil.   physique rid from its abscess: robed in saffronia

in the sky the evening star nudes itself and offers its pallid pelvis
thunderhead: tight scrotum.   my wheat sunders in his fine white teeth

[slightly foetid. foetal and stooped. an afterbirth of rags]

a song of Lazarus of Bethany

slightly foetid.   foetal and stooped.   an afterbirth of rags
myrrh-soaked pus-stained the cracklings the matted hair
but having heels.   I flushed out from my mortared vacuole

then the coins were lifted from my eyes: my lord
because holy is the viscera.   he seals me waxen
plenary dermis: unbroken and unblemished
once more in the trunk and legs orbicular   yet

am I not dust?   when I move through the world
the air receives me.   as did the dirt.   as does his kiss

[the heavenly noise of domesticity murmurs in the kitchen: *clink*]

a song of the last supper

All love is dead, infected
With plague of deep disdain

—*Sir Phillip Sidney*

the heavenly noise of domesticity murmurs in the kitchen: *clink*
plates are cleared and stacked on the sideboard.   desserts shimmer
taking coffee black: antidote to the drowse of too much wine

use it up wear it out: ain't nothing left in this old world I care about
a damasked table surrounded by bachelors.   some already parted
regimens of azt, d4t, cryxivan, viracept and early slumber

across the table a handsome bearded man.   his foot glances your shin
you'd sink with him beneath the empire mahogany: lift the perizoma
receive the host: his wounds.   your faith: the sash around his waist

[not a waking mutter. the locusts in cessation]

a song in the garden

not a waking mutter.   the locusts in cessation
redstarts dozing and nightjars silent in the tree hollows

longing perches on every branch: acacia myrtle poplar
and a sudden rush of wind kisses with its rough lips

even in the midst of this green and flowering grove: buttonwood
tamarisk silverking and rue.   paradise seems a vacant spot

only the poppies do not slumber: their calyxes turned upward
bid me drink.   and the dove from its secret place cries out

where is my bed?   where is the house in which I was conceived?
am I to lie here among thorns among brambles.   until the daybreak

let me hide: a spring in rock.   let me drink at that hour abundantly

[because I were ready before destruction. bearing the sign of his affliction]

a song of Simon the Cyrene

because I were ready before destruction.   bearing the sign of his affliction
in my laggard arms: the sign was made as the stretching limbs of him

oh, my chasms were afraid of this wooden place and sang over it:
"loose liver, mouth, roots, member"   a bellowing about our head

then we came to rest in the trees as in the end.   there should blossoms be
indeed I hang thickly upon him.   where clear heavens may breathe upon me:
all darkness, all comprehensible night.   let me be humbled in his abundant eyes

I shall want that the drinklings speak upon his heart: his dewy breast
for they have been vinegar and bitterness enough.   ravens among the wheat

"the carrier" I was called.   so did I carry: my hand did not defect.   my sores
who can tell us all about love: a flaying.   the sting of gall upon a hyssop reed

I am putting on his robe.   I clothe his sinew and drape from it and he loves me
here is the garland that moves not upon our head: impales.   razor thorns

and as that crown sits firmly so I sit firm.   and if everything should perish:
as bridegroom reckoned in his likeness I go.   rock, river, permeable flesh

[listen mother, he punched the air: I am not your son dying]

a stabat mater

listen mother, he punched the air: I am not your son dying
the day fades and the starlings roost: a body's a husk a nest of goodbye

his wrist colorless and soft was not a stick of chewing gum
how tell?   well a plastic bracelet with his name for one.   & no mint
his eyes distinguishable from oysters how?   only when pried open

she at times felt the needle going in.   felt her own sides cave.   she rasped
she twitched with a palsy: tectonic plates grumbled under her feet

soiled his sheets clogged the yellow BIOHAZARD bin: later to be burned
soot clouds billowed out over the city: a stole.   a pillbox hat   [smart city]
and wouldn't the taxis stop now.   and wouldn't a hush smother us all

the vascular walls graffitied and scarred.   a clotted rend in the muscle
wend through the avenues throttled t-cells.   processional staph & thrush

the scourge the spike a stab a shending bile the grace the quenching
mother who brought me here, muddler: open the window.   let birds in

[the ice hadn't cracked. stingy ground: frozen with its hoard of bulbs]

a song of the resurrection

the ice hadn't cracked.   stingy ground: frozen with its hoard of bulbs
how long would march flail us.   bastinado of wind and hail

one morning I rose.   declared an end to winter   [though cold persisted]
convinced that the dogwood wore its quatrefoil splints of convalescence

because the land gives back.   I wanted warmth within its chilled pellicle
radiating blades of *cordgrass* and *wild rye*.   the demure *false boneset*

on the phone with mary my friend: she too persuaded of the thaw
so long withdrawn a blindness had us.   desensitized to sneaping frost

we set out for the bluffs.   surely clover pullulated along the crest
and the air   [no longer chiding]   would teem with monarchs

I had word of a marigold patch: the welkin dotted with butterflies
orange blaze: the deceit of wings and the breeze's pulmonary gasps

the journey stretched.   why hurry?   the promise of the garden enough
the road a pleasant shifting through riparian forest: a windlass a wander

already I have taken a long time to tell you nothing.   nothing awaited us
nothing sprouted out of the ground and nothing flew about the bluffs

brown twigs: a previous splendor born to another season.   now swealing
the wick had held its brief flame: sodden.   the earth received it

whitetails foraged what was left of vegetation: we startled them grazing
one cardinal held watch at the empty beds: injury in the stark white trees

in the town a church kept bare its cross: draped with the purple tunic
we knelt to the wood.   and this I tell you as gospel: the sky shuddered

a bolt shook our hearts on the horizon.   for what seemed an eternity
[for we knew eternity by the silence it brings]   void: then scudding rain

—for Mary Szybist

[Α Και Ω]

a song of the undead

the sepulchre cleaves.   he loosens from the wall and flies
children assemble to him and he whispers "suffer"

this appetite for blood: he enrooted us to
lapping at the wounds upon his sullied fell

now he's scared of pine: the way it pocks his fair skin
in an arcosolium upon a slab he rests his weary teeth

bats flit through the lunette and adore him: blind angels
bridesmaids in black habits.   lifting the veil: *feed*

[came a voice in my gullet: rise up and feast. thunderous]

a song of Simon Peter, concerning his dream

came a voice in my gullet: rise up and feast.   thunderous
a vestment dropping from the violet cope above
not a vestment: a vessel.   amphora the shape of lips

vessel of skin moiled and swollen: a fretting leprosy
and why would I wish a taste?   inside, all manner of beasts
creatures covered in scall charbon and quarter evil

the sea-things one discovers in the net and tosses back
& the coney the camel the tortoise the hare the swine
oysters as well as snails.   those without fins or scales

though I hungered as a sick lass with her empty box
I could not be filled.   not with the tainted reasty lot
in my bowels a raven ruffled its dismal neck and cawed

now I was devout and nothing common or dirty
inside me: not a wild meat not a fruit or spice exotic
for I was a stone: washed in the stream.   I was cut clean

still the air split with want.   the urgent voice seized
because these *are* the pleasures of the world.   *eat*
of the glands I tasted many.   hearts.   lights.   pluck

what had been circumcised fit me.   the uncircumcised too
for nothing was given for my body which was not sacred
the seed the root the tongue and pure blood that cleanses

[when he comes he is neither sun nor shade: a china doll]

a second song of John the Divine, as at the end

when he comes he is neither sun nor shade: a china doll
a perfect orb.   when he comes he speaks upon the sea

when he speaks his voice is an island to rest upon.   he sings
[he sings like france joli: *come to me, and I will comfort you.*   when he comes]

when he comes I receive him in my apartment: messy, yes
but he blinds himself for my sake   [no, he would trip, wouldn't he?]

he blinds *me* for *his* sake.   yes, this actually happens
so that the world with its coins with its poodles does not startle

I am not special: have lied stolen fought.   have been unkind
when I await him in the dark I'm not without lascivious thoughts

and yet he comes to me in dreams: "I would not let you marry"
he says: "for I did love you so and kept you for my own"

his exhalation is a little sour.   his clothes a bit dingy
he is not golden and robed in light and he smells a bit

but he comes.   and the furnace grows dim.   the devil and the neighbors
and traffic along market street: all go silent.   the disease

and all he has given me he takes back.   laying his sturdy bones
on top of me: a cloak an ache a thief in the night.   he comes

[coda & discography]

a song of paradise

to enter that queer niteclub, you step over the spot: sexworker stabbed
reminds me of the chalk outlines on castro street or keith haring's canvases

missing.   beaten.   died at the end of a prolonged illness.   a short fight

phantoms of the handsome, taut, gallant, bright, slender, youthful: go on
the garment that tore: mended.   the body that failed: reclaimed

voyeurs, passion flowers, trolls, twinks, dancers, cruisers, lovers without lovers

here is the door marked HEAVEN: someone on the dancefloor, waiting just for you:

> *so many men, so little time* [miquel brown]
> *calling all boys* by the flirts.   patrick cowley's *menergy*
> *only the strong survive* [precious wilson] or *I will survive* [gloria gaynor]
>
> the flirts' *passion* and roni griffith's *desire*
> *the boys come to town* [earlene bentley]
> gloria gaynor's *I am what I am.*   eartha kitt's *I love men*
>
> *runaway* [tapps].   *seclusion* [shawn benson].   *helpless* [jackie moore]
> eria fachin *saving myself* and the three degrees *set me free*
> *goodbye bad times* [oakey & moroder].   *keep on holdin' on* [margaret reynolds]
>
> oh romeo's *these memories* and *the heart is a lonely hunter* [bonnie bianco]
> real life's *send me an angel.*   *earth can be just like heaven* [two tons of fun]
> yaz: *situation* and *don't go.*   and *why* by bronski beat

give me just a little more time [angela clemmons]
unexpected lovers by lime and *mercy* by carol jiani
let's hang on [salazar] and *maybe this time* [norma lewis]

vivien vee's *give me a break* and her haunting *blue disease*
ashford & simpson's *found a cure.*   *doctor's orders* [carol douglas]
sylvester singing *body strong.*   sylvester singing *stars*

About the Author

D. A. POWELL is the author of two previous books of poems. His awards include the Lyric Poetry Award from the Poetry Society of America, the Larry Levis Award from *Prairie Schooner*, *Boston Review's* Annual Poetry Award, a Pushcart Prize, a Paul Engle Fellowship from the James Michener Foundation, and a grant from the National Endowment for the Arts. Powell has taught at the University of San Francisco, San Francisco State University, Sonoma State University, Columbia University, and the University of Iowa. He is currently the Briggs-Copeland Lecturer in Poetry at Harvard. Together with Katherine Swiggart, he edits the online magazine *Electronic Poetry Review*.

The text of *Cocktails* has been set in Minion, a typeface designed by Robert Slimbach and issued by Adobe in 1989. Book design by Wendy Holdman, composition at Stanton Publication Services, St. Paul, Minnesota, and manufactured by Thomson-Shore on acid-free paper.